Thank you Eric for opening the door.

Thank you Alex, Jade, Gillian, Jennifer, Anthony, Izzy, Imogen and Franc.
This book is the result of your collective intention,
creative energy and support.

Thank you for this magical journey.

The Peace Intention Handbook
- The StillFlow way to Peace

First Edition

By Freya Lawton

www.thepeaceintention.org

ISBN:978-0-9575127-4-0

It's Time

This isn't the first book that's offered to help you change your life. It may, however, be the first that could save it or indeed save all of our lives.

The information shared has been spoken by many voices throughout history. The message in this book, echoed through the many quotations, come from a diverse range of people, across thousands of years, yet all sharing the same eternal message. That we are the creators of our own reality.

I'm simply adding my voice to many others and sharing the teaching and realisations I've received. It appears that this message wants to be heard, simply perhaps, because we have not yet heard it. This was made clear to me when I was writing this book at a friend's house in Rome. Stuck for some wording to explain a point about judgment, I wandered over to a bookcase and randomly selected a small book from the hundreds on the shelves. It fell open and as I read the words, I realised that they perfectly described the point I was making. Their author was Marcus Aurelius, Emperor of Rome 161 to 180 AD, known with good reason as the last of the good emperors. Before that moment I'd never even heard his name, and yet across thousands of years, he was handing me the words I sought.

Thankfully, there's a growing number of voices today sharing the message. Each encouraging our collective 'aha moment,' as we remember who and what we truly are and recognise the responsibility and opportunity that offers us to change our lives and change our world. Many of the ideas and techniques in this book may well be familiar to you from other sources, but their common intention is to remind us that we are not separate, that we are aspects of one single energy field and that our thinking determines the quality of the whole of our experience.

My intention in naming StillFlow was simply to make this information easier to find, to live and to share.   Once something is named it becomes real. It can be talked about and passed on to others.

Throughout time, this wisdom has been ignored and suppressed, distorted and even burned, but today things are different. Today we've created a greater need than ever before for it to be heard and acted upon quickly. Luckily, we've also created the technology by which it can be shared with others by the click of a computer key. It's up to us now, you and me, to share it with our friends, our neighbours, our family and total strangers alike.

To act upon the opportunity that StillFlow offers us has never been more urgent.

This isn't about becoming perfect. Whilst facing the challenge of writing this book, I've forgotten every step at least once. It's my intention though, to spend more time remembering to live the StillFlow way each day.

It's in your hands now.
Much Love

Freya Lawton
Founder of the Peace Intention &
Author of 'The StillFlow way to peace'

The world as we knew it has changed... forever.

Science is confirming the ancient wisdom
of the spiritual teachers.

We truly are ALL ONE.

Everything, you included,
is part of a single energy field.

Thoughts and intentions are powerful,
creative forces that are right now shaping your life.

You now have the opportunity to create peace
in your life simply by changing your thinking.

How will that bring peace to the world?
Your inner peace not only affects your own life,
it directly impacts on the world around you.

Have we ever even dared to dream that each of us might be
the creator of world peace?

It's time to begin...

peace in you = peace in the world

*"Very little is needed to make a happy life;
it is all within yourself, in your way of thinking."*

Marcus Aurelius, Emperor of Rome (AD 121-180)

What is StillFlow?

It's all about changing your mind about the way 'reality' works!

StillFlow is a practical way of being that makes sense in a world where everything is energy, an energy that responds to your thoughts.

StillFlow is not a 'spiritual' path or a personal development fad, it's a reasonable and intelligent way to make positive improvements in our own lives so that we can improve the world around us. StillFlow is not new, it reflects an ancient wisdom that has been voiced (but perhaps not heard) throughout human history. If it is the way you're already living, then use it as a reminder, or better still, use it to share your understanding with those that may be hearing these ideas for the first time.

Living the StillFlow way can help you improve every area of your life:

- Developing inner peace
- Improving relationships
- Dealing with money issues
- Improving self confidence
- Overcoming fears and phobias
- Assisting health issues
- Increasing creativity

StillFlow isn't just about improving our own lives, though. It also offers a new understanding of how we can influence the wider world issues we once felt powerless to change, simply by choosing to see how StillFlow changes our own lives.

Change you = change your life = change the world

Considering living the StillFlow way makes sense when we absorb this vital piece of information. That absolutely everything in the world, ourselves included, is actually just energy.

Ancient spiritual texts have been telling us for thousands of years that everything is part of one unified energy field, but now, for the first time in human history, scientists are having to agree. For the very first time both science and spirituality are coming together to tell us the same story about the nature of 'reality' and the ways in which it works.

Scientists are also finding proof that the energy that creates our world actually responds to our thoughts and intentions. In a very real sense, this means that we can actually influence our own reality. Some people might find that hard to believe or accept, and no-one is asking you to believe it. Why would you? Think of StillFlow as a personal experiment that offers you the chance to see what happens when you make practical use of this knowledge for yourself.

It offers you the chance to see for yourself whether you can change your world and the world around you simply by changing your way of thinking.

How Do You Live
the StillFlow Way?

Pay attention to the 'vibe'!

In the 1960s they used to talk about the 'vibe' when someone or something felt good or bad. It turns out that in a world that's purely vibrating energy, the 'vibe' is a very real thing.

Each of us is a unique energy centre that both emits and receives a constant flow of invisible vibrations to and from everyone and everything around us. When we are thinking, our thoughts can create emotions that either raise or lower the vibration we're emitting.

It makes sense to talk about emotions having high and low vibrations when we recognise that that's exactly what they are - energy vibrating at lower or higher frequencies. Emotions like happiness and joy emit high vibrations whilst anger, sadness, anxiety and the like, emit low frequency.

Living the StillFlow way is all about understanding how we create our vibration and doing what we can to make it higher. Not just because a higher vibration feels so much more enjoyable, but also because everyone around is affected by our vibration and the life we experience reflects the vibration we are transmitting.

StillFlow is about recognising that our emotions are the result of our thoughts and the thoughts that create low vibration emotions are simply the result of our past experiences and our

9

personal beliefs. It helps us to see the damaging effect that hanging onto or justifying low vibrations has on us and everyone around us. Once we recognise that our low vibrations aren't being caused by what's happening to us but are the result of how we're thinking about what is happening, we can choose to let these low vibrations go rather than hang onto them. We can also see that the force behind our low vibration emotions is actually fear and that ultimately we only need to let go of one thing, our own fear.

Once we do that we improve our experience of the moment, we raise our overall vibration and this, in turn, draws to us people and experiences that reflect our higher vibration. Then we experience the need to judge situations or other people as wrong less and less frequently. Ultimately, as our fear lessens, we come to experience more and more peace in our lives and more and more acceptance of everyone we meet and everything we experience. Basically, it's a win:win situation.

So StillFlow is about experiencing for ourselves how raising our vibration not only improves our own life and that of everyone around us, but also changes the vibrational influence we have on the entire world! More importantly, it gives us a way to release our fear and the judgments that they create.

So how do we start to change our vibration?

Take Responsibility
for How You Feel

If everything is energy responding to your thoughts, does it make sense to feel you're a victim of circumstance in any way?

No?...Congratulations!...You're now a fully empowered, conscious creator of your own life.

Peace is within your grasp.

You now have the opportunity to take responsibility (NOT blame!) for what you've created so far and have the power to change anything you wish to change from now on.

You are now in full control of your life experience!

Notice Negative Thoughts

"When you realise how perfect everything is you will
tilt your head back and laugh at the sky"
The Buddha

We used to think our thoughts were just personal things that affected nothing and no one but ourselves, but it turns out they are the exact opposite. They are actually powerful electromagnetic transmissions that effect everything and everyone around us.

If the life we experience is simply a reflection of our thoughts then it's vital that we start to notice what we're thinking and to respect our thoughts for the power they have to create our lives.

As we send out these thought transmissions, the universal energy field from which everything is created responds to bring into our lives whatever we have focused our attention on.

We could interpret this to simply mean negative thoughts will attract negative experiences and people, and positive thoughts the opposite. So if you live the StillFlow way you simply decide to pay attention to your thoughts and to notice whenever you have a negative thought about anyone or anything...yourself included!

To start with, simply recognising that there's an actual link between what you think and what you experience is a huge leap in changing your reality.

To live the StillFlow way you must begin to treat your thoughts as the instructions that the universe receives in order to shape your life - because that's exactly what they are!

Think of your brain as a computer that sends instructions out into the world to give you exactly what you ask for, and of your thoughts being the programmes that are running the computer. Become aware of the programs (thoughts) you're running. Is your thought making you feel good or bad about yourself, someone or something else?

Let go of negative thinking

As a first step, whenever you notice that you have a 'negative' thought you can add an additional couple of words on the end of it: "Delete that". You can say it out loud or say it silently to yourself. The important thing is to make a habit of saying it. It may sound mad but this simple phrase has the power to cancel out the negative programme (thought). By noticing your negative thought and consciously choosing to delete it - you're clearly stating your intention to cancel that instruction to the universal energy field (after all, 'delete' is a thought too!). More importantly you're becoming consciously aware of how your thoughts are affecting your emotional state and how that state, and how that state is influencing your life experience.

Consider where negative thoughts come from

It's one thing to just notice when you have a negative thought and delete it but the next step is to understand where the negative thoughts are coming from in the first place.

Each of us has a huge set of beliefs that's unique to each and every one of us. Most of us assume that everybody else shares, or at least ought to share, our beliefs. It's often quite a shock when we discover the truth...THEY DON'T! Everybody else has their own unique set of beliefs formed from their own life experience, many of which aren't the same as ours. It's the basis of conflict the world over.

You may or may not even be aware of most of your beliefs because we don't tend to spend time reviewing or considering them. That doesn't mean they are unimportant though, far from it. Our unique set of beliefs creates a filter through which we perceive the world and everyone in it. Our beliefs tell us how the world is, or at least how it ought to be! However invisible they may be on a day to day basis, our beliefs are the fundamental drivers of our life experience. They're the source of our thoughts and so, ultimately, are responsible for how we react to the world and how we feel about our experience of it.

Becoming aware of our beliefs is a fundamental part of StillFlow. We don't analyse them or judge them though, we just begin to observe their powerful influence over our life experience.

Each of us has unique beliefs about:

- The way the world works;
- How the world should be;
- How we and perhaps, more importantly, how other people should behave;
- What we think of ourselves and what we can and can't do, our strengths and our weaknesses.

As we view the world through our personal belief filter we find ourselves in a state of constant judgement as we analyse how well the world is measuring up to the expectations our unique set of beliefs is creating. When the world appears to be in sync

14

with our beliefs, all is well.

When it isn't though, when things don't appear to be the way we want them to be, believe they should be or hoped they would be - in short when we're judging that something is WRONG - it can trigger uncomfortable emotional reactions (a low vibration).

BELIEF creates NEGATIVE THOUGHTS/JUDGMENTS which then create a low vibe EMOTIONAL STATE.

So our unique set of beliefs is not only creating our thoughts and ordering up our life experience, it's also the source of all of our negative emotional experiences.   Once we start to notice the negative thoughts as we have them, we'll also start to notice the beliefs that are creating them.

But what if we're right, what if something really is wrong?

If everyone has different beliefs, then clearly there's never any single truth that something is objectively right or wrong, only our perspective, based on our own unique set of beliefs. In any situation we judge to be wrong, there's going to be an opposing view that thinks it's right. It is simply our own experience and our own beliefs, our own 'stuff' if you like , that causes us to make a particular judgment. We have to ask ourselves: What do I want more - to be 'right' or to live in peace?

One thing we can be sure of is that trying to change someone else's beliefs is an almost impossible task. What StillFlow offers instead is a powerful way for us to change the world around us simply by letting go of the judgments we're making about it.

Now that we know that it's our own belief system that's the source of our negative thoughts and low vibration emotional states, we have to ask what we gain by hanging onto those beliefs. Is it possible that we could just as easily decide to let it go instead? That is the essence of living the StillFlow way; taking personal responsibility (NOT BLAME) for observing our beliefs and the way in which the role they play in creating a lack of peace in our lives. StillFlow is all about 'letting it go'.

In understanding life the StillFlow way we empower ourselves in every moment to recognise that we're creating our own low vibration experience and to know that we can either hang on to it or let it go. StillFlow empowers us to make that choice. Then we have the chance to see for ourselves what happens when we let it
go as opposed to hanging onto it, to observe the change we feel within us and the change we observe around us.

Whether or not we can accept that this will change things, it's only in actually practicing living the StillFlow way that we'll know if it makes a difference to our lives. It's not a philosophy, it's a practical way of living. If you don't try it, you'll never know if it works.   If peace in you and peace in the world is a potential outcome of giving it a go - isn't it worth a try?

What lies below?

What's tricky is that many of our beliefs are subconscious, that is, we don't notice them on a moment by moment basis.   In fact, much of the information we use to get on with our lives is subconscious. We don't often have to sit down and remember the thousands of small movements and muscular adjustments necessary to make a cup of coffee, it just happens. The same can be said of beliefs. They mostly function invisibly, affecting our behaviour and influencing our lives without us even knowing it.

That doesn't mean we can't begin to notice their power to make us think negatively. Once we know that we have them, we can observe our own reactions and notice when we start to fall into judgment. The important thing is to recognise as often as you can how the judgmental thought is making you feel. Then it's up to you to decide if you want to let go or to hang onto it and continue the negative low vibration you're feeling and transmitting into the world. As long as we're paying attention to our negative / judgmental thoughts as they arise, we'll begin uncovering these hidden beliefs.

Stop Blaming Anyone or Anything for How You Feel

If we accept that everything in our lives is directly reflecting our own thoughts, then we also have to accept that any challenging person or situation that shows up in it is part of that reflection. That means that challenging people have to turn up in order to show us what we need to let go of.

Before, we would have thought it was the person/situation that was MAKING US FEEL a low vibration (anxiety, anger, self-doubt and so on) but now we know how energy works, we know that the challenging situation itself is actually being CREATED BY OUR own thoughts and the underlying beliefs that create them.

That means:

Firstly, that the challenging person or situation HAD TO TURN UP because we are carrying some belief that energetically drew them/it to us

Secondly, that the only way we can continue to be challenged by it/them is if we choose to hang onto our judgment that they're somehow wrong or to blame them for making us feel the way we do.

Most importantly, that by choosing to recognise that our discomfort is just the result of our past experience and the beliefs we've developed, knowing that there's nothing to be gained (other than more of the same) by hanging onto it, we can transform our experience in an instant. If we choose instead, to consider that we have created that person/situation IN ORDER TO FEEL our discomfort, that everything that's happening is perfect, we can simply choose to let it go. As we let it go we release the low vibration we've been hanging onto, our vibration rises, we feel better and in a very real way...WE LITERALLY RISE ABOVE IT!

Remember that if we fall back into the old way of thinking and continue to believe that we're just hapless victims of circumstance, there's no way to break the loop that we're creating. There's no way the people that we think are MAKING US FEEL that low vibration can stop cropping up. It's just the way energy works.

If we justify how we feel by saying "This always happens to me", we're absolutely right, but it does so only because of the way we're thinking and we have the opportunity to change that now.

With StillFlow anything we would once have blamed for causing our discomfort now becomes an OPPORTUNITY to let go of the underlying beliefs that caused them to show up in the first place.

We do that simply by noticing our thinking, by letting go of judgments, and by letting go or Clearing our negative thoughts and low vibration emotions.

Choose to See
Everything as Perfect

*"There is nothing in the world either good or bad
but thinking makes it so"*
Hamlet, William Shakespeare

Once we start to see how our personal beliefs, and the judgments they lead us to make, are creating our low vibrational emotional reactions, we're presented with a great opportunity. We can now choose to see everything as perfect, just as it is. Suddenly, the idea that everything is happening for a reason begins to make some sense.

We don't have to believe it straight away though. StillFlow is all about experience. From the StillFlow perspective, we can choose to live as if everything were perfect in order to see what happens when we do. The more we notice how things change around us when we let things go the more we can see that things aren't happening to us randomly but because of us, because of the vibration we're carrying. Then we start to see for ourselves how the thoughts, beliefs we are carrying around and the resulting low vibrational emotions they create in us must inevitably draw to us experiences and situations of a similar vibration. Again, this doesn't on any level mean it is our FAULT. That implies it's because of something we have done wrong so we deserve what we get. The StillFlow way is to recognise this as an opportunity for great transformation in our lives. Once we start practising living the StillFlow Way it becomes obvious which option creates more peace in our lives.

So why does this mean everything is perfect? Because suddenly difficult situations that would once have been challenging become opportunities to let go, to release ourselves from the beliefs that were drawing the challenging situations to us (or causing us to see them that way) in the first place.

You could see life as a spiral journey. In the old way of thinking we're spiralling down as we move through life, each rotation getting smaller and smaller as our beliefs limit our experience more and more. The 'negative' experiences and old beliefs of the past drawing to us more and more experiences of a similar vibration. The more similar experiences we have, the more our old beliefs are justified.

A great example of how this begins is the young pupil discussing his future options with the careers advisor. The youngster shares his dream of becoming an astronaut only to be met with disdain. "Don't be ridiculous, you had better have a rethink. That's just not going to happen. Take a look at these business studies leaflets". The careers advisor, living in a smaller spiral than the young man, is passing on his limited beliefs, not out of spite but because he's seeing the world through his own limiting filter. Perhaps he even believes he is saving the young man from the pain of disappointment. Perhaps, he too, once had a similar hope but was met with ridicule when he revealed his dream. The young man, embarrassed and disheartened by the advice, decides it's an impossibility and that he must never mention it again, let alone pursue his dream. He leaves the room with a powerful new belief that he may well carry with him throughout his life. That life is not for you to live, it's for you to compromise. Through time, the accumulation of the limited beliefs of other people can cause us to spiral down in our expectations of life.

StillFlow though, is all about reversing that trend and beginning to spiral outwards, creating a larger and larger experience of life as we first recognise, and then let go of, the limiting beliefs we have come to live by. When we live the StillFlow way we can transform anything we would previously have considered a problem or a challenge into an opportunity to let go of the real cause of what upsets us – our own old stuff. Once we stop blaming the outside situation for how we feel and look inside ourselves for the belief that's filtering our experience and causing our suffering, we're fully empowered to let it go. Old memories, beliefs or judgments, all of it can be let go, and in doing so we can create both a state of peace within us and a renewed sense of freedom and possibility in our lives.

That would mean that there are no more difficult situations or people only opportunities to let go of what caused us in the past to experience them in that way. It gives us the chance to let go of the old stuff, safe in the knowledge that once we do, we can change the vibration that was previously drawing challenging situations or difficult people into our lives.

Could you see everything as perfect? Are you at least willing to give it a try and see for yourself how this understanding changes everything?

Choose to 'Let it Go'

So, it's all very simple then, you simply let it go. But how do you let it go?

A lot of living the StillFlow way is about creating an entirely new way of thinking about how life works, based on the fact that everything - you, me, the chair, anger, joy and absolutely anything else you care to mention - are all vibrations of energy. Given this new understanding, things that in the old way of thinking would have seemed impossible to do, suddenly seem like the only sensible thing to do. What if we only think we can't let things go because we have been told it's not possible, that it's just another (limiting) belief we've picked up from other people - one that we now know we can choose to let go?

In order to begin letting stuff go, we first have to re-examine the idea that someone or something is making us feel the way we do. In what we can call the old way of thinking, we were taught to believe that certain people and situations inevitably make us feel a certain way. That's how most people still think: "I feel sad, mad, jealous etc because of what so and so did or said, or because of what just happened." Living the StillFlow way, we can choose to think very differently, in a very different way. We consider that what's happening had to happen in order to create the perfect opportunity to LET GO of the belief that resulted in the low vibration we experience in that particular situation.

Let's take an example to make this a bit clearer. You go to a party with your new partner and as soon as you arrive at the party s/he goes off and starts chatting to an old girl/boyfriend. They stay there most of the evening and when it comes time to leave you find you're feeling really angry, jealous, sad - fill in whatever emotion comes to mind as you imagine the scenario. The old way of thinking is that you're justified in feeling the low vibe emotion because of what they did to you or how you imagine other people interpreted what they did. In this old way of thinking they MADE YOU feel bad because of what they did.

The StillFlow way of making positive use of that experience would be to begin to recognise that because of the way the universe works, the partner HAD TO go off and spend the evening with their friends BECAUSE YOU NEEDED TO FEEL sad, mad, jealous or whatever because your belief system held the potential to feel that way. It wasn't what your partner did that made you feel that low vibe, it was your own beliefs that caused you to JUDGE the situation as wrong or bad. We assume that ANYONE would feel the same and that also justifies how bad we feel.

Living the StillFlow way, we would notice as the low vibe emotion and accompanying judgmental thoughts started to arise, and we would choose to simply let them go. We would stop BLAMING our partner for how we felt and start thanking them for the opportunity to acknowledge and let go of the true source of our low vibrational emotion, our own beliefs about the way the world should be.

This is really important because it stops you doing something which makes it very hard to let go of stuff - justifying it! If no-one and nothing (you included) is TO BLAME for how you feel it makes it much easier to choose to let it go, particularly when doing so makes it far less likely that a similar situation need occur in future.

This is key to StillFlow.

Letting it go is not about seeing yourself as a better person, as somehow superior because you can let it go. It's also not about being passive or allowing people to do and say whatever they want to. It's about understanding the mechanism of attraction that draws experiences to us. Letting it go makes sense not just because it changes our experience in the moment but because it changes what happens next. It lessens the strength the limiting belief has to shape our future experience. It may sound bizzare, and you will have to try it and see it for yourself, but people and situations can be changed in a moment once we begin to let stuff go. The more you release, the more you change your filter on the world and begin to see the world with new eyes. As you let go of judgment your vibration rises and you begin to create a different reality in which you no longer draw to you the challenges you once experienced.

It may take a while to get into this new understanding but the more you do it, the easier it becomes. It's even possible to get to a point where it seems laughable to hang onto feelings of a low vibration. The more you practise responding to situations the StillFlow way the more quickly you will find yourself letting stuff go. After all, it's just an experience and it can be as short lived as you choose it to be, now that you know the world is simply reflecting your own vibration.

But how? We still come back to how to let it go.

Again, it's all about the context in which you are experiencing something. The more time you spend choosing to explore living the StillFlow way the more obvious it will become to you what it means (and how simple it can be) to LET IT GO. Before you get started though, it may still seem challenging to just let something go. The difference is, now you have in your belief system the idea that you COULD let it go. That changes everything. Before you started reading this that possibility simply didn't exist. Now that it does, you are already living in a new reality, one in which letting something go isn't just possible, it's sensible both for you and everyone else. Suddenly, letting it go makes sense.

We all know the difference between hanging onto something and letting it go. We've all let go of stuff before and felt that instant state of relief as we did so. Letting it go isn't some admission that you were wrong or that we are a doormat, to be walked over or treated badly. It is simply a new level of understanding that acknowledges the simple way in which we create our own reality. It's the sensible choice when we know the benefit it will bring and that the consequence of not letting it go is...more of the same.

Remember to follow the logo:

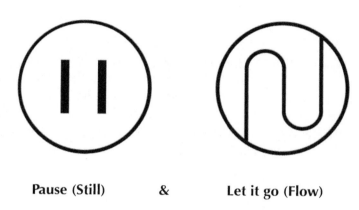

Pause (Still)   **&**   **Let it go (Flow)**

It's always your choice but if you choose to hang onto it and keep justifying how you feel, there's really only one thing that can happen ... something similar will have to happen to you AGAIN! The old belief and the low vibe you are hanging onto will simply draw to it another opportunity for you to feel it and release it. The events may look different and the people involved may or may not be the same, but you will draw to you a scenario that again produces that same old low vibe experience and it will do so again and again UNTIL YOU LET IT GO.

So if it doesn't feel good...let it go!

Energy Clearing -
Your New Superpower
(Accelerated 'Letting it Go')

The thing about letting it go is that, first, you have to be feeling something to let go of. That means you have to wait until you're in the situation or with the person that triggers your discomfort and only then can you choose to let it go. Sometimes things happen so quickly though, that you get overwhelmed by your emotions in the moment and it just isn't possible to let it go there and then. You get lost in the old way of thinking and start to justify how you feel. So, luckily, with StillFlow, that's not the only way to let it go.

You can start using your SUPERPOWER. You know, the one you were born with but didn't know that you had, until now!

You have the ability to clear energy frequencies.

It's called energy Clearing and it is an incredible way to make positive use of the knowledge that everything is energy that responds to your thoughts and emotions.

It's a simple but amazingly effective technique that has an unlimited number of applications.

In essence, energy Clearing is the process of actively directing your thoughts and intention to release limiting beliefs or low vibrational emotions. As there's a proven link between negative thought processes and illness, Energy Clearing is also a way of releasing the harmful thought processes before they begin to create ill health.

28

Why does Clearing work?

One way of looking at it is as a step up from using the 'delete' technique. What you were doing then was taking control of the fact that your thoughts create your reality to cancel out negative thoughts. Energy Clearing involves going a step further to direct your thinking to neutralise the energies (thoughts or emotions) that are bothering you.

If everything that exists is just energy vibrating at a specific frequency, then that includes your emotions and your beliefs. StillFlow recognises that the unified energy source that shapes itself into your life experience responds to your thoughts and intentions. That means that if you actively choose to focus your intention to release the limiting belief or low vibe emotion, the world of energy must respond accordingly...by releasing it for you.

Start Energy Clearing

It's all about intention!

You can use the energy Clearing process on yourself, on other people, and even on situations. It's free, it's safe and it does the the person doing the Clearing as much good as the person being cleared. In fact, it's most powerful when you have a group of people Clearing together.

At first, it's best if you find a comfortable space where you won't be interrupted, but even if you are, you can just go straight back to Clearing. You can do Clearing anywhere and any time...on the train, at work, in the park - wherever you want. The only thing that really matters is that you take the time to actually DO IT!

There are a few ways of going about Energy Clearing and you may find that one suits you better than the other.

Clearing a situation or relationship

STEP 1) Decide what you would like to clear

Take a moment to think about what's been happening in your life recently. What's been bothering you? What has been lowering your vibe? What or who are you finding difficult or challenging? It could be something you regret or want to forget. It doesn't matter what it is and it doesn't matter what the cause is, the important thing is that you decide what it is you want to clear.

Remember, from the StillFlow perspective any situation or person that's bothering you can only be doing so if you have some existing belief that is being triggered by it/them. So Clearing isn't about fixing other people or forcing a situation or a person to change. It's simply about recognising that the world 'out there' is just reflecting our own beliefs and judgments (our stuff) and focussing our intention to let clear whatever old stuff is causing us to be bothered by it/them. Once we do this the situation/relationship will change in alignment with our clearer response to it.

STEP 2) State your intention to yourself

Say to yourself a few words that clearly state the intention that you have.

For example,

"clear any anxiety around my exam tomorrow"
or
"clear my relationship with John"

There's no way to get this wrong and there's no special way you have to say it. Just make it the focus of your attention.

STEP 3) Sit quietly & notice what you notice

Once you've stated your intention to clear stuff, simply pay attention to the many ways in which the movement of energy can be noticed in the body. You don't need to try and force anything or make anything happen - once the intention is stated the energy will start to move. Hold the intention clearly and try and stay as neutral as possible...just notice.

You may want to close your eyes while you do your Clearing.

It's often easier to focus on your intention and to notice the subtle energetic changes with your eyes closed.

Obviously DON'T close your eyes if it could be dangerous!

There's no way to get Clearing wrong and although it may sometimes seem as if nothing at all is happening, stay with it for at least a few minutes and just remain aware of what you're experiencing. Noticing energy can be a very subtle process at first but the more you do it, the more you start to learn your own inner energy language.

You may notice emotions coming up or flashbacks to old experiences, you may notice physical symptoms in your body. If you notice anything, try not to get caught up in it at all, just let it pass. Stomach rumbles, burping, yawning and eyes watering are all common signs that energy is releasing. It's all fine... just old energy moving.

Also, remember that your intention is powerful regardless of whether you notice anything at all. It's a positive statement to the universe about what you want to happen next. Instead of blaming someone or something else for what you've been experiencing you're instructing the universe that you would like the relationship or situation to be cleared, to be lightened.

What you are actually Clearing here is YOUR relationship to the situation or person. You are instructing your subconscious to release the limiting beliefs or judgements you have about it. You may not know what those beliefs are, you don't have to, your subconscious knows what you are asking it to do.

At some point you will feel as if the Clearing is over. At this point you may notice that you feel a little lighter or that there's a sense of stillness. It may be that you have only cleared some

32

of the issue and there is still more to let go. Ask yourself if there is more to clear and trust the immediate yes or no answer to get. Trust your intuition here, you know the answer to this question. If there's more to clear then repeat the process. It may be that you've cleared all you can for now and need to come back to it later.

If you're Clearing with someone else it can sometimes be interesting to tell them what you noticed. It doesn't matter if it makes sense to them or not, and there's no need to get hung up on what you notice. All that matters is that you've let go of some old stuff that's no longer useful to you.

Clearing an emotion

Sometimes we just get the low vibration emotion without any clear idea of what's triggered it. In this case you can simply focus your intention to clear the emotion that you're experiencing. It could be irritation, anger, anxiety, self doubt or another emotion. Focus your attention on the feeling that you want to let go of. It may not even be something you are currently experiencing but you may have been bothered by it recently. In this case simply focus your intention to clear the emotion and follow the steps above.

Clearing yourself on a regular basis

Making Clearing a regular part of your day or week can be hugely beneficial. Spending just 10 minutes Clearing yourself before you go to bed or in the shower or on the bus to work can make all the difference to your day.

You don't have to be specific about what it is you want to clear if nothing particular comes to mind. It's also beneficial to just hold a general intention such as

"Clear me of any low vibe emotions" or "Clear any negative thoughts"

It may seem a little strange at first but the more you do it, the more you'll begin to notice both the beneficial effect and the subtle inner signs that low vibrations are being released.

Clearing stress

Stress is a common experience, especially in today's fast-paced world. It's also a very broad description for a variety of symptoms. You may experience stress as a feeling of being over-stretched, having too little time, being hypersensitive or over-emotional. All of these can be helped with Clearing. Again, you don't need to know the exact cause of your stress, the important thing is that you take the time to Clear the symptoms you experience as often as you can.

Clearing symptoms

From an energy point of view all symptoms, physical, psychological or emotional are in some way the result of a disruption to the person's energy field.

If you, or someone you know, has symptoms they're struggling with, you can use Clearing to release the old stuff that may be creating it. Obviously, don't suggest they stop any conventional medical treatment, but Clearing and the energy connection it creates between you can be a way of creating a sense of wellbeing within them.

While bringing your attention to yourself or the person with the symptoms, hold the intention to release whatever's at the source of these symptoms, or simply to release the symptoms themselves.

Clearing fear

At the root of many of our limiting beliefs and the low vibrational emotions they can create in us, is the vibration of fear. One of the most effective ways to use Clearing is to focus your intention to Clear that fear. You may not be experiencing fear or even think of yourself as being a fearful person but fear is in all of us and can show itself in all manner of limiting and judgmental beliefs. The more we intend to Clear fear from ourselves the more our vibration rises.

Clearing is unlimited

You can use Clearing to release anything that comes to mind. You can even use it to Clear the energy in your home or workplace, as low vibrations can affect the energy of spaces too. Use it on your pets or other animals. There really is no limit, just use your imagination and focus your intention.

Clearing with a friend

The more people get to know about StillFlow, the more effective it will be for all of us. So don't keep it to yourself, introduce a friend to the StillFlow way and the energy Clearing technique. It's more beneficial for everyone when we sit down to do some Clearing together, rather than getting involved in a discussion about problems. If stuff comes up for you, choose to clear it rather than talk about it or get into the imagined rights and wrongs of the situation. After all, now that we know that our thoughts and emotions create our reality, it makes sense to just LET IT GO!

If you decide to do some Clearing with a friend - you don't have to wait until you have time to physically get together to do it. Because of the inter-connectedness of all things you can TUNE

IN to each other from anywhere on the planet. The connection will be just as strong.

Making it a regular thing that you do not only benefits both of you, but also creates an even deeper level to your friendship.

Create a group

Why not introduce a group of friends to the StillFlow way of seeing things and try Clearing together? Working together to clear stuff can be much more powerful because the unique frequency of each person in the group means they will be able to clear different stuff.

Putting StillFlow at the heart of your way of being allows you to offer a far more effective way of dealing with issues that come up for members of the group. Again, you don't have to all be in the same place at the same time to work as a group. You could just set up a regular time each day or once a week when you all tune into each other and clear whatever needs clearing for each of you.

If someone gets ill, or experiences a hard time emotionally, you could all just choose to tune in and clear for them. As a group you also have a powerful opportunity to focus your intention together to clear personal, local or worldwide conflicts.

Your group can be as big or small as you choose. Inviting new people to join means the whole group can share their understanding of how StillFlow works and how it's made a difference in their own experience. Again, these could be local friends or people you know through the internet. You'll also find details of local groups on the www.thePeaceIntention.org website.

Visit energy power sites

The world is littered with the remnants of a long lost age when humanity understood the power of invisible energy lines that criss-cross the planet. They understood that these energies emanating from within the earth have a powerful effect on our health and wellbeing. They also recognised that these sites, often marked by standing stones or stone circles, have the potential to amplify and carry our thoughts and intentions across the planet. You may find that you are drawn to take your group to visit one of these sites to focus your intention make world peace a reality. Along with your personal commitment to The Peace Intention by living the StillFlow way, establishing a local group and visiting these ancient sites are two of the most powerful things you can do to contribute to world peace.

As well as visiting your local power sites, you might want to look further afield. You'll find details of organised physical and virtual Peace Intention power site visits on www.thePeaceIntention.org website.

Let go of Needing to be Right

"Everything we hear is an opinion, not a fact.
Everything we see is a perspective, not the truth."
Marcus Aurelius

Another important element of StillFlow is to ask ourselves why it's so important to be right about things? More importantly, why do we need other people to admit that we are right? It's a fundamental part of expecting other people to share our beliefs and part of the old way of thinking.

Now we know that each of us has a unique set of beliefs and that everyone else has a unique perspective too, needing to be right makes no sense. Add to that the realisation that it's the best way to create conflict and a resulting low vibe – what's the point of it?

Even in the world of science there are many different points of view. Even the things that have been agreed upon at one time as scientific fact will be superseded by new understandings. Just as the science of the time once believed that the world was flat, or that the sun revolved around the earth, our perception of scientific 'truth' constantly changes.

If we can never know anything other than our own truth, why does our truth need to be shared by others? If we have information or experience that works for us, we can share that with them (that's exactly what's happening now). But if they don't accept it or don't want to hear it, that's perfect too (as everything is). Convincing someone that we are right and they are wrong is a very different thing from sharing possibility. You will know when you have crossed the line, you will begin to experience some sort of low vibe emotion such as frustration, irritation or even anger.

If you find yourself at that point, you now have the chance to let those low vibes go. That's all that matters. After all, from a StillFlow perspective, the only reason someone turned up in our reality to disagree with us, was to allow us to feel the resulting low vibe emotion and give us the opportunity to let it go. Not so we could give in or back-down, those are part of the old way of thinking. Ironically, you will find that once you let go of the need to be right people will be much more willing to hear what you have to say. You may even find you can hear their point of view as well, both potentials much more likely to create a peaceful outcome.

Again, also in the words of Marcus Aurelius,

*"Reject your sense of injury and
the injury itself disappears."*

Consider Why Some People 'Bother' Us More Than Others
(The Power of Resonance)

'If we learn to open our hearts, anyone, including the people who drive us crazy, can be our teacher.'
Pema Chodron

On a very basic level we tend to like people that are like us not necessarily in personality, but in terms of a similar belief system. Sharing a similar outlook on life tends to make for a less confrontational relationship. It's easier to like people that are a bit like us it's more difficult to like people that aren't. It's not uncommon though, for even the strongest of friendships to end over a disagreement.

There's more to it though. Sometimes people don't even have to open their mouth for us to feel uncomfortable around them. We might even describe them as having a BAD vibration. Quite rightly, the language we use actually reflects exactly what's going on between us energetically.

As we've said before, each of us transmits our unique vibration and picks up on, or receives, the vibration emitted by other people.

We could imagine the vibration we transmit consists of the many smaller vibrations of each of our beliefs, thoughts, memories and emotions. It is, in a sense, our unique frequency which represents our current state of who we are energetically.

When we feel uncomfortable around someone it is actually because we have something in common with them. We both share a similar vibration. Somewhere in their vibrational pattern is a vibration we also are carrying. As we spend time around them these similar vibrations will start to resonate together and we will begin to feel a discomfort. In the old way of thinking we would believe it was something about them. Now though we know something in them is resonating with something in us.

That doesn't mean that we are LIKE them personality-wise. It is only a small part of us but importantly it is coming from within us. This is the reason we all interact differently. Someone that makes one person feel good may make someone else feel a low vibration. It's all about the way the vibrations interact between us. Similar vibrational frequencies will resonate together.

With StillFlow, of course, we know now that they offer us a wonderful opportunity. Whenever we feel uncomfortable around someone we can choose to change the way we react to the experience. Instead of doing what we would have done before, in the old way of being - moving away, avoiding them or BLAMING them for how we feel, we can choose instead to simply notice how we feel when we're around them (or even when we think about them) and let go or Clear our low vibration response. This benefits both us and them at the same time.

This is one of the most powerful ways to experience StillFlow and the opportunity it offers to create peace in our lives and in everyone we meet. This is key to understanding the chain reaction our thoughts create in the world. The next time you feel uncomfortable around someone try responding the StillFlow way. Take a moment to pause and follow the StilFlow logo. Be (STILL), notice how you feel and let it go (FLOW). Keep doing it until you notice the negative feeling leave you, until you reach a point of stillness and neutrality. Now observe that person again, notice how you feel about them now. More importantly notice how they seem in themselves, what they say and do. Do they seem different now?

See the World as a Mirror
(Yes, It's All About You)

'We don't see the world as it is we see it as we are'.
Anais Nin

Is it possible that some of the judgments we make about other people are simply reflecting the beliefs we have about ourselves? If you look at things the StillFlow way - the answer is YES and that creates another opportunity!

We all have parts of ourselves that we find hard to accept, behaviours or traits that we've been taught are unacceptable or undesirable. If we want to know what they are, we only have to take an honest look at the judgments we make about other people. Often, when we judge something in ourself, instead of acknowledging it we become sensitive to it in other people. Again, it's about perception as we are actually projecting it onto someone else.

Again the beliefs that fuel this projection and cause us to judge other people are part of our unique filter on the world. They aren't objectively TRUE they are just part of our unique point of view. Again, we may assume everyone shares them, but often they don't. Our beliefs are ours alone and when we use them to judge other people we are simply lowering our own vibe.

Everyone does it or perhaps we should say everyone did it until we realised that by doing so we are simply creating our own low vibe experiences, again and again. Before we realised that we could let go of these judgments and improve not only our own lives but that of everyone around us by doing so.

Make Friends With Your Inner Critic

We've talked a lot about judgments we might feel towards other people and situations, but low vibrational emotions can also be triggered by that little voice inside our head that criticises us. It's the one that tells us we aren't good enough, slim enough, fast enough or clever enough....the list goes on....and on.

This inner voice is the most significant voice we ever hear. No matter what other people say to us they can't counter our own inner voice. It's after all the voice of our own beliefs. Whether we want to hear it or not, it voices the beliefs we have gathered from other people and from our experiences along the way. Only we can choose to let those beliefs go and quieten the voice of our inner critic.

The dialogue with our inner critic or our voice of limitation can be dealt with and let go of in the same way as criticisms we make about other people.

First, we recognise that the inner critic isn't telling us the objective truth. It's just repeating some old belief we picked up long the way that we now realise we're better off without. It doesn't matter where it came from, it's simply not helpful! What does matter is that we realise it's just old stuff and we have the power to LET IT GO! We also realise that the self-criticism reflects the beliefs (programs) that we're putting out into the world to create our own reality. If we don't change the programme we'll simply continue to create situations that reinforce the belief. We either stay trapped in this loop or we choose to free ourselves from it.

Remember, the voice of our inner critic is only relaying our limiting beliefs. It's not true!

We can use 'DELETE THAT' every time the voice criticises us.

We can notice the voice but choose to say LET THAT GO NOW!

We can also spend time every day focusing our intention to Clear the specific self-criticisms we've developed over time.

Don't Make a Drama Out of...
Well... Anything

If emotions are just energy vibrating at different frequencies, doesn't it make sense to take them a bit less seriously? Doesn't it also make sense to stop thinking that we own these emotions? After all, we don't think we own a song we hear just because we hear it and it makes us feel a certain way. We know in a sense it's an artificial reaction. It doesn't mean we can't enjoy our emotions for a while. StillFlow isn't about becoming an emotionless zombie but it is about allowing low vibe emotions to pass rather than clinging onto them and justifying them. That's what you might call making a drama out of them.

Our emotions allow us to have an extraordinary range of experiences and the world would be a very different place without them. But it's easy to get very caught up in our emotions, often hanging onto the low vibes for way too long, probably because we had no idea of the negative influence they would have over the future we were creating.

Japanese scientist Dr Masaru Emoto's pioneering research showed the effects our emotions have on water molecules. He divided a water sample in two and then attached the word LOVE to one and HATE to the other. He then froze them and looked at individual molecules of water from each sample under a microscope. The crystal structure of the water sample given the word HATE appeared to be disfigured, while the sample given the word LOVE was symmetrical and beautiful. This research is a huge leap in our understanding of how our thoughts effect our physical wellbeing. Especially when you consider that around 70 percent of the human body is actually water! This is the effect your low vibes are having on you and anyone they're directed towards!

Dr Emoto also carried out fascinating experiments with growing rice. This time he divided a quantity of rice into 3 equal amounts and placed each into a container with some water so that the rice seeds could sprout.   One rice sample was subjected to positive emotions by the researchers on a daily basis. The second sample received an equal input of focused negative emotion. The third sample was simply ignored. The results confirmed those of the water experiment. The sample which received the positive input sprouted first and grew the most strongly and the sample that received negative emotional input sprouted less quickly and grew less strongly. Most significantly of all though, was the discovery thtat the sample that was completely ignored sprouted last and grew weakest of all. This may have something very important to tell us about why we create drama in our lives.

If you look on YouTube.com there are many people who have replicated this experiment with the similar results in their own homes.   You may want to follow their example and try it for yourself. After all, StillFlow is not about accepting things blindly it's about trying it for yourself.

So why all the drama?

The results of Dr Emoto's rice experiment offers an insight into why some people create drama in their lives. It may also go some way to explaining why we all have a tendency to hang onto negative emotions longer than we need to.

Clearly, many people have never really had much positive attention (love) in their lives and, in such a hectic world, many people struggle to receive much attention at all. But like Dr Emoto's rice seeds, we all need attention (energy) from other people in order to stay alive. As we know, when we put our attention towards something there is a flow of energy towards it. We're all intuitively aware when someone's attention, and the energy flow associated with it, is being focussed towards us and we are equally aware when it is taken away. Perhaps this is how we know when someone is staring at us from behind. Even though we can't see them, we can feel the energy flow.

Just like the rice seeds, we flourish when we're given positive attention from other people. But if we grow up without it and only recognise negative attention (energy), perhaps we intuitively know that this is better than no attention at all. Hanging onto low vibes and justifying why we feel them and making a bit of a drama out of them in order to gain some attention - could be seen as a sensible behaviour when we recall how badly the rice that was ignored did. But it's only sensible if you don't realise that your own negative thoughts and emotions are drawing more and more low vibe experiences towards you. Once you know that, you can change things and create the chance to experience truly positive attention, not just from other people, but more importantly, from yourself.

Don't get involved in other people's drama

When someone we know goes into a DRAMA about something, it's expected that we will somehow empathise with them and agree that they have somehow been MADE TO FEEL the way they do. But it just doesn't make any sense to carry on supporting other people in doing this when we know how energy works. That doesn't mean we have to judge them for the drama or not recognise that they may be having a low vibe experience but we can change the way we respond to them. Instead of collaborating in their drama by justifying why they feel bad we can offer them an alternative way of understanding their experience. We can step away from joining in with the drama and explain why we are doing so. They may not like it - because it's not what people expect - but in doing so we offer them a positive alternative, a new way of being that could help them experience more happiness and joy in their lives.

We can share the StillFlow way with them or offer to show them how to do some Clearing of the old beliefs and emotions that are really creating their situation.

Don't forget though - if what appears to be someone else's drama brings up low vibe stuff for you (for example you get angry, frustrated or exasperated with them) then you must let your own stuff go first and foremost. After all, there's no point showing other people how to live the StillFlow way if we are forgetting to do it ourselves! Sometimes letting our own stuff go is all that's needed to free them from what appears to be their drama.

Quit Worrying
(Forever)

When you know how your thoughts and emotions affect your experience, worrying enters a whole other level of useless activities.

If you haven't really thought about what worrying actually is, it's your brain telling you something negative, usually about something that hasn't happened yet and that it has absolutely no way of predicting.

In a way, your brain is trying to keep you safe. It thinks that the worry's a useful strategy and up to a point it may well be. It might prompt you to remember something you'd forgotten, it may cause you to be better prepared but after that it simply drains your energy and wastes your experience of the present moment, lowering your vibe into the bargain!

Worrying thoughts become the focus of your attention and they create a low vibe emotion which not only effects how you're feeling in the moment, it also energetically influences what you draw to you in the future.

So, as always, don't judge yourself for worrying, it's just an old way of being. Don't try not to worry, it wont work. Resistance will simply make it stronger. Instead, acknowledge the thoughts, notice the emotional reaction you have and let it go. Remember whenever you can to see things from the bigger picture, the picture you create by living the StillFlow way. You may want to hold the intention to Clear whatever beliefs are creating the worrying thoughts but either way – let it go.

With StillFlow you're releasing the belief that is creating the worry. In this way you are freeing yourself from having a similar reaction to similar situations that might come up in the future. You are, in a sense, reducing your capacity for worrying, regardless of the situation.

Live Beyond Limitation

What are you capable of? Is it something you've thought much about? Is it possible that we have all been living within the limiting beliefs we have picked up throughout our lives that we've never really stopped to ask ourselves the question? Have you ever wanted to do or be something and been met with the words 'you can't do that!' either from someone else or coming from inside your own head? Obviously, those words are pretty powerful. Mostly, we listen to them and believe that they're right. Often we are too scared of humiliation to even try to defy them.

Now though, things are different. What if we decide we're creating the opportunity to hear these discouraging remarks from ourselves or other people, just so we can let go of our own belief in them? After all we wouldn't take notice of what was being said unless on some level we actually believed it was true.

The beliefs we have that determine the boundaries of what we think we're capable of can be described as limiting beliefs. We all have them. Some of us have far more of them than others. Shaped by our life experiences and what we are encouraged to believe by those people who most influence us, our unique set of limiting beliefs sets the expectation for our lives. Or it did until we started living the StillFlow way. Now we know we have the power to start to live beyond the limits of these beliefs, simply by recognising they're there and choosing to let them go.

We can choose to let them go because we now know they're just 'old stuff' that we've picked up somewhere along the line. Again, once we start to become aware of these thoughts we may well be surprised at just how many limiting beliefs we're hanging onto. We may still have the memory of an uncomfortable experience when we tried something new. Or we may be hanging onto something a friend or relative told us when we were younger. What we were told and taught when we were younger can hang around and limit our lives for ever, without us even realising it, if we let it.

But now we know that this is just old stuff and it will only continue to limit our lives as long as we choose to let it.

The world we've created together is just as much a product of limiting beliefs as our individual lives. The process works the same way. It's only once we start to examine the beliefs we live by that we can see how limiting they are. Absolutely everything that determines how we live our lives has arisen out of someone else's belief. The limitation of our world is the product of our collective limiting beliefs.

Are you living your life or someone else's?

To some extent we are all living someone else's life because we are viewing the world by beliefs we've been taught or have picked up along the way. StillFlow gives us the opportunity to change that by examining our personal and collective limiting beliefs and letting go of the fear that prevents us from stepping beyond their limitation.

Now that we're noticing our thoughts and seeing the underlying beliefs that create them, we can choose to let them go. As we become more and more aware of our own thinking and the power it has to create, or in this case limit, our experience, we can choose to observe and let go of these limiting thoughts as and when they arise. We can choose instead to create positive thoughts and intentions that acknowledge no limit to our potential.

Tune into the Power Frequency Gratitude

Gratitude is something of an abstract concept until we start to pay attention to it. It's something we may experience at certain times, but very few of us choose to make the deliberate experience of gratitude an intrinsic part of our lives. Why would we?

Well, in StillFlow, gratitude is a shortcut to directing your energy to a higher vibration. It's easy to get caught up in the past or worrying about the future but taking a moment every now and then to look at the amazing things that you've already created in your life is a great way to come back into the present moment and move instantly into a higher vibration. There's always something to be grateful for even if it's simply for being part of the extraordinary experience we call LIFE.

The more often you take the time to feel grateful, the more you'll recognise the shift that occurs as you move into that higher vibrational state. You'll become more familiar with what the vibrational frequency we have named gratitude, feels like. The more you focus on gratitude the easier it will become to shift into that higher frequency whenever you choose to. It will become as easy as re-tuning the radio to a different station. Becoming familiar with this higher state will eventually be all we need to live the StillFlow way. Instead of needing to Clear or let go of each low vibrational emotional reaction as we feel it, we can instead retune our vibration to the gratitude frequency as soon as we notice it has slipped to a lower vibration.

The frequency of gratitude also has a very powerful part to play when you move to the next level of StillFlow which is focusing your thoughts to create the life you want to live.

Consciously Create Your Life
(With the Power of Intention)

**Positive intentions + Positive feelings
+ Positive action = Positive outcomes**

The wonderful thing about letting go of old limiting beliefs and the thoughts and emotions they create is that it offers you an incredible opportunity. It enables you to start using the power of intention to create the life you truly wish to be living.

Until you let go of those old beliefs though, they'll carry on actively running the show, drawing to you the type of experience that resonates with them. Even if you try to set new goals and intentions, if they contradict your existing beliefs they will not be strong enough to overcome the existing programmes you are running.

So does that mean it's a waste of time trying to intend a new life for myself unless I have let go of all my old limiting beliefs?

No, it doesn't, because StillFlow recognises that one of the best ways to uncover your existing limiting beliefs is to start setting new goals and intentions. It's like a red rag to a bull to that inner voice. It just can't wait to tell you why that new goal isn't possible or why that latest intention will never happen. That's fine from a StillFlow perspective though, because once you entice the old limiting beliefs out into the open, up into your conscious awareness, you can start to let them go. Only then will your new goals and intentions take over to steer your life in the direction you want it to go.

Think of your life as a boat adrift on the sea. If you don't know where you want to go, how are you going to get there? If all you know is where you don't want to go and your limiting beliefs are focusing your thoughts on that, how will you end up anywhere but where you DON'T want to be?

When you bring together your thoughts about how you'd like your life to be with a high vibrational emotion, you create a powerful force, an INTENTION. Suddenly your boat has a rudder to steer it and a motor to power it. So what would that emotion be? Yes, the power frequency of gratitude. The one you have been practising and learning how to tune into as often as you can. This is the 'other' important role of gratitude, powering our intentions.

For many years we've known that positive intentions work. In fact, many years ago, a young man called Napoleon Hill was asked by Andrew Carnegie, one of the wealthiest men in the world, to write a book about creating a successful life. He was asked to interview many successful people and ask them to explain exactly how they lived their lives. Carnegie was convinced that they were all doing the same thing, that in fact, there really was a recipe for success.

After many years, Hill's book Think and Grow Rich was published and the results confirmed Carnegie's suspicions. There were indeed common habits and behaviours that all the rich and successful people shared.

Consistently, those who were considered to be living a successful life:

- Set clear goals (intentions) for themselves

- Wrote them down and focussed on them regularly

- Behaved as if the intentions had already come true!

StillFlow adds a couple of extra pieces to the jigsaw...

- Start small. Practice the intention process by thinking of something small that you'd like to experience or change in your life

- Tune into the gratitude vibration when you're focusing on your intentions

- Notice your limiting beliefs which your inner voice will kindly start relaying to you the moment you set your new intention

- When you notice them, write them down too...they are VITAL! These thoughts are telling you what programs you are already running in your mind computer that have so far prevented you from having or achieving whatever it is you have set down as your intention.

- Let the limiting beliefs go or actively Clear them. After all they are just old echoes of an old way of thinking and are on their way out if you're living the StillFlow way

- Imagine that your life is an ongoing film and you are Directing it as well as having the staring role. Whenever you are concerned about what happens next, remember that you are the Director, you choose what happens next!

- Consider that you are not trying to change your current reality, you are simply creating a new one that reflects your intention

- Take positive action...it's not just about how you think...you also have to move towards your objectives in a positive way

- Look out for coincidences and signs that mean something to YOU. It doesn't matter how surprising they may be or how insignificant they appear to other people. If they mean something to you - act on them. Your head may want to dismiss them as unimportant but they are intuitive clues leading you towards your intention.

Navigate With Your Heart
Instead of Your Head

One important way to take positive action towards your intention is to get out of your head and into your heart.

Although we have language that suggests we all know we have a heart intelligence 'listen to your heart', 'follow your heart' etc we aren't really encouraged to actually believe in it, let alone to listen to what it tells us. In a world that has come to rely almost exclusively on our limited head intelligence for logic, reason and hard facts the heart's communication through intuition, inner knowing and coincidence are often dismissed as illogical nonsense to be disregarded in favour of 'the facts'. In recent years though, a research institute in America, The HeartMath Institute, has scientifically proven that your heart actually does have its own form of intelligence. It has also shown that there are more communication channels running from your heart to your head than the other way around.

Experiments have also been carried out that prove the existence of intuition. The results may not make logical sense in our old way of understanding the world, but it all makes perfect sense in a world where everything is energy. We've come to believe that for us to know something, we must have experienced it for ourselves. We must have learned it, read it, heard it or been told it. Information about it must in some way exist in our own head.

Heart intelligence doesn't work that way. The biggest difference between heart and head intelligence is that heart intelligence is not limited to what we personally know. Instead, the heart appears to act as an antenna with unlimited access to whatever it is we need to know.

The famous psychoanalyst Carl Jung described this infinite pool of knowledge as the collective unconscious. In the old world this would have seemed impossible. How can we know what we don't know? But in the new world of StillFlow where everything is understood to be part of one energetic source, where nothing separates us from each other or from anything else, suddenly this begins to make some sense. Suddenly, from this new perspective, the question becomes, how is it possible that we can NOT have access to whatever knowledge we need or want to know?

What if the only thing that's stopped us accessing this pool of knowledge is the collective, limiting belief that we can't do so? What if learning to navigate by the heart could re-activate the heart antenna and allow you to access it whenever you choose? What if our heart antenna never stopped working we just stopped listening to it?

Why listen to your heart?

Choosing to listen to your heart may be one of the fundamentally life changing decisions you ever make. It has the potential to open up a spontaneous, creative, inspirational flow that seems to come, not from within us, but instead seems to flow through us.   When you start to listen to your heart, you start to live with less fear and limitation and more love and trust.

Your heart is able to perceive a much, much bigger picture than the brain of what's going on and how you and your life is interconnecting with everything else that's happening. In contrast, the brain in your head only works with what you already know or have already experienced. It knows nothing at all of the infinite inter-connectivity that exists beyond it.

Here's one way of thinking about it. Your heart intelligence is a little bit like your own 'flying eye' helicopter, high in the sky taking a bird's eye view, reporting holds-ups on the roads ahead and suggesting the best route to take while your head though is sitting in the car with you, obsessed with following the map, simply unable to see what's up ahead. Because of that, it often goes into worry mode.

Listening to your heart can be a tricky thing to start doing. We have all become very dependent on the rational, logic of our brain. Making logical, reasonable decisions, based on what we already know, is what we expect from each other. It's the logical thing to do, or it was in the old way of thinking. We want things to make sense, to seem rational and no-one wants to feel foolish. Ridicule is a very powerful tool that we use to keep ourselves and each other living within our collective limiting beliefs. Once we truly understand the significance of the inter-connectivity of all things though, everything changes.

What if the route your heart suggests is the route to a more magical, joyful, expansive life? After all, there are many people who believe that your heart intelligence is a kind of magnet that pulls you towards your life's true purpose and allows you to break free of the confines of limited thinking to create a very different kind of reality.

Which would you prefer to follow?

As was said earlier, your head speaks of caution whilst your heart speaks for joy and expansion. Maybe it made sense in the past to rely solely on the cautious brain. But if we live the StillFlow way, we know the quality of our future is dependent not on random chance, but on the our own thinking. We know we have nothing to fear. Whatever happens will be perfect and we can choose to respond to challenges by seeing them as opportunities to let go of the old beliefs that drew them to us. We're no longer victims of circumstance. We're conscious creators of our own experience, intending our own reality and accessing the wisdom of the collective unconscious to lead us towards it.

What does your heart sound like?

- Your heart speaks quickly, in a flash, with certainty and then gets shouted down by your doubtful head intelligence.

- The first voice is your heart, the one your head will try to tempt you to doubt

- Your heart's messages may not seem achievable, logical or sensible to follow - your head's will

- Your heart will tell you things your head will doubt you know

- Your heart in moments where you 'just know' what to do - your head will speak through long drawn out and often stressful internal dialogues where it tries to work out what to do

- Your heart will speak in silence and in moments when you're alone

- Your heart communicates with synchronicity and signs that only you will recognise.

- Your heart will answer if you ask it to help you.

- Your heart is waiting to speak to you!

Other Ways to
Raise Your Vibration

"The quieter you become the more you can hear."
Ram Dass

Spend time alone, in silence

Something special happens when you choose to spend time alone, especially when you resist the urge to fill the space with any man-made sounds - no music, no radio, no TV, no reading, no nothing... just you and the universe. That's you, too.

When the artificial noise is turned down, you'll start to hear things more clearly. You'll notice what your head's thinking and more importantly you'll notice what your heart is feeling. You may well notice great resistance even to the idea of deliberately spending time alone in silence, perhaps because we know we'll find it uncomfortable to be alone with our thoughts and emotions.

Living the StillFlow way though, we can use the silence as an opportunity to allow our thoughts and emotions to show themselves. We can then notice them without judgment or justification and choose to let them go.

In this way, the decision to be alone in silence becomes a deliberate choice to grow and release our lower vibrational emotions so they no longer create discomfort in our everyday lives. In this way what appears to be 'nothingness' is transformed into a positive experience. Silence is transformed from an empty space into a very powerful tool for personal transformation.

Let it out

While you're spending time alone in silence and not taking anything IN, start letting stuff OUT. While the TV and music are turned off and you're not filling yourself up with the noise and words of the outside world, take the opportunity to let your own thoughts out.

Write them down, speak them to yourself, record them or draw them. You don't need to judge them or worry about what they "mean" or if they are right. Just let them out. Listen to yourself and hear what you have to say. Start to notice if what you are writing is coming from your head or your heart.

Let nature help

If you're able to spend time alone in nature, that's even better! The vibration of the natural world is very high and can clear low vibrational emotions incredibly effectively. Walking alone in nature with the intention of letting go of low vibrations (you can be specific if you choose) can be a powerful clearing experience.

More than this though, see how you feel when you dare to speak to nature. We have been taught that nature is inert with nothing to say as it has no intelligence of it's own, after all we don't hear it speak out-loud. Many ancient and indigenous cultures though, respect every element of nature as a conscious manifestation of the same energy source that creates you or me. For them, it is perfectly sensible and reasonable to ask advice from the trees or seek the wisdom of the creatures. This wisdom will not be heard out loud though. The answers to your questions will be received through your heart.

As well as speaking with nature look for and acknowledge symbolic messages it brings you. Again, as with coincidence, this information will be of significance to you and may seem irrelevant to others, but if it is meaningful to you, that's all that matters.

Ground yourself

When did you last take your shoes and socks off and walk or just stand barefoot outside on natural ground such as grass or earth? Research suggests that this has a powerful rejuvenating effect. It releases the negative effects from a wide spectrum of electromagnetic radiation, from computers, mobile phones & masts, radio & TV broadcasts, WiFi, Bluetooth, power lines, domestic wiring and other electrical appliances.

Swimming in the ocean or natural sources of moving water like rivers or streams will have a similar beneficial effect.

Notice what you consume

Once you begin to notice your own vibration or recognise what it feels like to do Clearing, or notice the difference between hanging onto or letting go of a low vibe, you become ever more sensitive to the energy of everything around you. After all, everything around you has it's own vibration which is inter-connected to your own. By becoming aware of these vibrational frequencies we can make intelligent choices about the things we do and don't do. We can pay attention to the things we consume and those we choose not to consume. In this way, we understand how everything we consume becomes a part of our own vibrational frequency, in a very real sense.

Everything, from what you eat and drink to the music you listen to, the films and TV programs you watch, how much time you spend in nature, the books and magazines you read, the News you watch and the papers you read and even the people you spend time with, they all influence your vibration with their own. So do mobile phones and WIFI signals, which can affect your personal energy field in a detrimental way.

You might want to make sure you use your mobile phone sparingly and don't leave it switched on by your bedside overnight. You may even want to consider looking into one of the orgone products that you can wear or carry to protect your energy from the ever increasing array of vibrations that interfere with your energy field, especially if you live in a city. You can even use orgone products to improve the frequency of your food before you eat it.

The thing is simply to become aware of how things affect you. Do they make you feel a higher or a lower vibration?

StillFlow and
Unconditional Love

*"Your task is not to seek for love but merely to seek and find all the
artificial barriers you have created within yourself that you have
built against it."*
Rumi

When you start to live the StillFlow way, you do something
incredible. You step out on a journey towards unconditional
love, a state of unconditional acceptance that most people have
no idea even exists. It's a state so far removed from the kind of
conditional, hormone charged, romantic love we're taught to
expect, that it's incredible the two even share the same name.

So is it possible, that by living the StillFlow way we might
experience moments of unconditional love towards strangers
and friends alike? If you really think about what you're doing,
you're moving away from the judgment that's so inevitable in
the old way of thinking, where we see everything and everyone
as separate. As Rumi describes in the quote above, StillFlow is
a way of consciously removing the artificial barriers (old beliefs)
that previously prevented you from accepting yourself and
everyone and everything as perfect.

Once that process occurs, a greater experience of love is the
inevitable consequence. No more enemies, no more strangers,
no more barriers, just the unconditional acceptance (love) of
ONE.

Healing You Heals Other People

"The only thing that truly heals is Unconditional Love."
Elizabeth Kubler Ross

By letting go or actively Clearing any discomfort we feel towards other people, rather than blaming them for causing it, not only do we clear it from our energy field, we also clear it from theirs. Simply because it is all part of the same energy field. So in a way, there is no 'mine' or 'theirs,' just the frequency we're experiencing as discomfort. So when we release our own stuff we're also benefiting other people. In some cases, this may be enough for them to appear to us as a very different person, as the barrier we felt between us is removed.

Peace Pilgrim

There was an extraordinary woman who lived in the USA. In her later years she gave away all her belongings and started walking across the country. She walked with a message of peace which she believed was ultimately created by acceptance. She never knew where she'd sleep or where her next meal was coming from. Often people would offer her a bed for a night or two. She often encountered dangerous situations but she believed that by acknowledging and releasing her own fear she would remain safe and more importantly her acceptance was transformational of others.

One night a truck driver invited her to sleep the night in his cab. She accepted even though she sensed that the driver had bad intentions towards her. Rather than give in to her anxiety she chose instead to let it go and accept her experience. In the morning, she woke to find the man crying. He told her that when he invited her into his truck he had intended to harm her but when he saw how trusting she was he felt something change inside him.

When we judge ourselves we often interpret the words and actions of other people as judgmental too. This can become a vicious cycle as we sink into a ring of self-hatred. We judge ourselves, so we expect others to judge us and we use that as a reason to judge ourselves even more harshly. The truck driver is just one example of this.

Somehow, in this experience, Peace Pilgrim was able to create a profound healing in the truck driver simply by choosing to let go of the judgment she initially felt towards him. Tears are often a sign that some deep transformation has occurred. Healing in this sense is a much bigger concept than the one we are used to. In the old way of thinking healing is concerned only with removing physical symptoms of ill-health or emotional or psychological imbalance. From the StillFlow perspective, where everything is first and foremost energy, we have to remember that beliefs and the thoughts they create are the starting point for the imbalance we eventually experience as symptoms.

This is the kind of healing potential that's possible when we choose to live the StillFlow way.

It's Time to Create
Our New World - Together

"Action is the antidote to despair."
Joan Baez

The real magic of StillFlow lies in the way it creates a fundamental change in the external reality we experience. When we let go of our judgments, not only do we feel better in ourselves, but the people or situations we once saw as problematic, are actually fundamentally altered. We don't simply see things as different, they themselves are different. This is something you have to experience for yourself, and it truly is magical.

In a way, it's as if we step into an entirely new reality, a world in which the old rules no longer apply.

It's been suggested that there's an infinite number of realities, or parallel universes, that exist simultaneously with our own. Perhaps what StillFlow opens up is an opportunity to direct reality so that we step into a new universe, one of our own choosing. By letting go of the idea that we and the reality we experience are fixed and unchanging, we begin to create a flexible, malleable reality where we move between universes as and when we choose to refocus our intention.

So is it possible now, for us to come together and make use of the opportunity StillFlow offers to create a new reality not just for ourselves but an entirely new world reality for all of us?

Stop protesting and start creating - (resistance is futile!)

In energy terms, anything you fight or resist can only get stronger. If your reality follows your attention, it's inevitable. The way energy works means simply that your negative experience of something will increase the longer and stronger you resist it. Remember that the energy that creates your life experience is simply a direct reflection of what is going on inside of you. Fighting against, protesting against, resisting stuff you think is wrong will simply exhaust you and strengthen whatever you oppose. It will meet your opposition with equal force, and you will be stuck in a situation of frustration and ever-depleting energy.

So does that mean we're powerless to change things? Does it mean we have to ignore what's going on in the world and just standby and do nothing just in case we fall into judgment or emotional reaction? No, it simply means that the way to change things the StillFlow way is to recognise the way that energy works and to flow with it.

Just as in our own lives we need to see what our limiting beliefs have created for us, we go through the same process collectively as humanity. Once we realise that low vibrational frequencies will always draw into our lives opportunities to feel them and let them go we can see that this pattern is occurring in exactly the same way in the wider world. Everything we see in the wider world that we would choose to change is occurring because of the limiting beliefs we are living by as a collective. After all, the world has been created by our thoughts and emotions, we just didn't realise what we were doing. Now we know though, we know that dwelling on the negative is not the same as acknowledging it and letting it go. We don't let go of our fears by pretending they don't exist, we do it by bringing them into our consciousness briefly and then choosing to let them go.

So whenever, we consider things we think are wrong with the world, we must let go of our own contribution to creating it. Notice what you react against, notice how you feel, let go of the negative response you have (after all it's coming from within you) and then turn your attention 180 degrees away from it and put your energy into a positive alternative!

There is always a positive alternative. If it exists already, find it and get involved, if it doesn't then you have the perfect opportunity to create it yourself and provide an alternative for others. It will be much more effective and much more fun.

It's about turning "Why don't they...?" into "Why don't I...?" or better still "Let's...".

Co-creation and collaboration:

We now know that we are all part of a single energy source. In real terms, that means there's nowhere that you end and someone else begins. We are literally all one. So isn't it about time we started working that way and realising that striving to achieve anything - success, power, money, fame or anything else, just for ourselves, might not be the way forward? Once we acknowledge our interconnectivity, we're all working for everyone. Everything we do affects everything and everyone else.

Once we begin to break down the barriers we've created within ourselves that have prevented us from experiencing this, everything we do is transformed.

It's time for conscious co-collaboration within ourselves, with each other and with the universal energy force that's ready and waiting to create the reality we focus on....

Once again, resistance is futile, so if there's something that bothers you, seems inadequate or limited, then you have the opportunity to get involved in creating something new. By holding the intention to be inspired with new ideas for new ways of doing things you may begin to get a feeling for something new. Remember to ask your heart not your head. In fact, you're asking the universe itself for inspiration and your heart is the receiver of the wisdom it shares with you. Take time alone, in silence, in nature if you can, and ask the question "What is the positive alternative to ...?' The answer will be shown to you. In fact, you already know the answer. You just forgot that you did.

Your new idea or new way of doing things will need other people's skills and energy to turn it from an idea into a reality. Set your intention to find the people to work with. They're out there just waiting to be called to work with you.

If your head starts to tell you that you aren't good enough or important enough to start something new, let that limiting belief go. There is NO-ONE and NOTHING more significant than you. You create the world. It's time to create the world you want to live in. Actually, it's time for us all to create a world we want to live in!

Give it away

Coming together to intend a new world means leaving behind many of the old beliefs that have caused us to create both conflict and competition. Most importantly, it means letting go of the fear that caused us to accept the limitation of these beliefs in the first place. Once we lose our fear of loneliness or of there not being enough to go around or that other people mean to harm us, we can start behaving in a very different way. We can move into a state of conscious co-creation. This is already happening across the planet as people move from fear into trust. Trust in themselves, trust in each other and trust in the universe to co-create our new reality.

Once we recognise the potential this new way of being offers us we can begin to give things away to others in a way that simply wouldn't have made sense from the old way of thinking. Resources shared with others are no longer just kind gifts, they are meaningful contributions to co-creating our new way of world together.

Giving it away doesn't just apply to resources it also applies to our ideas, our skills and our time. If you're a big ideas person and you have more than enough good ideas than you can handle, choose the one that you're most drawn to and put your energy into that. Then give the other ideas away to someone else. It's time to get over the idea that we can win whilst someone else loses. This idea is based on a concept of separation and competition that no longer makes sense. Our new world will inevitably reflect our new understanding that we are all one. We cannot truly succeed in isolation, not if we truly understand success. We only have to take a look at the deep isolation and sadness many of those that have 'succeeded' alone whether in monetary, business or fame terms to see that what we are missing is a natural expression of our interconnectedness. It is time to work together in the full understanding that by benefiting each others live we also enrich our own.

Give your skills and energy to positive things

Q: What are You Doing with Your Energy?

You may feel you don't have the time to give any energy to anything outside of your job right now. You may work long hours and feel drained at the end of the day. You may even think that you have little to offer.

What if it's not the job that is exhausting you but the feeling of disempowerment and lack of choice it creates in you? What if you're suffering from the inevitable result of living within the the confines of limited beliefs? When we look at our options in life, we begin to see how our collective belief system has created a world in which humanity is not encouraged to flourish but is expected simply to fit in. We go right back to the example of the young man and his visit to the careers advisor. Why couldn't he be an astronaut or, for that matter, a time-traveler or an intergalactic ambassador for peace? Because we have created a world in which that appears to be impossible. But we know now that impossibility is defined by our own limited thinking and our own fear and we can change it.

Whatever job you have, whatever you learned at school, you

have skills and abilities that can make a major contribution to creating our new reality. It may be hard at first to recognise these qualities if we've accepted the old limiting belief that our job, our career or lack of it is the sole measure of our worth. If we've learnt to judge ourselves only by qualifications and skills required for the job market - where we sell our time and energy to the highest bidder.   We may think we have left this belief behind and yet we may still find ourselves perpetuating the belief when we ask a stranger at our first meeting, "What do you do?"

What if we started to define ourselves by other qualities, human qualities, the type of qualities we value in each other outside the 'job market?' What if we started to ask ourselves and each other not "What do you do?" but "What do you intend?", "What's your passion?", "What brings you joy?", "What's your strength?"

What if we started to consider our sense of humour, our creativity, our joy of cooking, our love of gardening or walking, our love for children, our compassion and our many other attributes as what we have to offer, rather than the musty pieces of paper marked 'qualification'? In truth, we all have so much to give and there are so many waiting for us to give it.

Whatever little voice tells you that you have nothing to give or you have no time or you don't know where to start, LET IT GO and go out and make a difference. Doing something that makes you happy and joyful is one of the simplest ways to raise your vibration.

StillFlow &
The Peace Intention

Are you ready to make peace a reality?

The Peace Intention is a worldwide movement of people who recognise the vital role they play in creating world peace. This book is it's 'handbook' helping people create greater peace in their lives. The purpose of the Peace Intention is to offer a place where people can come together to commit to making peace a reality in their own lives and in the wider world.

It's underpinned by the understanding that everything we experience is part of a single, unified energy field and that our focused intention has the power to transform our reality. It's NOT a pressure group or a place to exchange information about the horrors of war around the globe. It's sole intention is to focus our thoughts and energy on what we DO want to create - PEACE. It's about a shared understanding that the only way to create Peace in the wider world is to create it first within our own lives.

StillFlow is the way in which the Peace Intention assists you in making more peace in your life and in the world. 'The StillFlow way' is the handbook of the Peace Intention. It's the process by which we can understand how we are creating our reality and gives us the tools and information to begin to change it. It helps us move from the judgment and resistance that create conflict to the acceptance that not only creates peace in us but magically transforms our external reality.

If you're ready to 'Make Peace a Reality' visit the Peace Intention at *www.thePeaceIntention.org*

Where you can:

- Join the Peace Intention

- Sign the Peace Intention Declaration, your personal reminder of your commitment to creating peace in the world by expanding peace and acceptance in your own life.

- Download the e-book of 'The StillFlow way to Peace' for yourself or to send to others.

- Buy hard copies of the book for family or friends or gifting for 'strangers'.

- Find out about StillFlow Clearing groups or start a group if there isn't one in your area.

- Discover more about orgone to assist in countering the vibrational interference of mobile phones and wifi signals.

World Peace
The StillFlow Way

"There is one thing more powerful than all the armies of the world. That is an idea whose time has come"
Victor hugo

Making a personal intention to living the StillFlow way is based on the understanding that we are all part of a single unified energy field, that there's no separation between what we perceive to be 'me' and what we perceive to be other people. Therefore, absolutely everything we think and feel affects absolutely everything and everyone in the world.

So, is it possible that living this way could bring about world peace? Well, let's face it, there's a lot more chance of creating world peace by living the StillFlow way than by living the old way!

The more peace there is in you, the more peace is reflected back in your world.

peace in you = peace in the world

By choosing to live the StillFlow way you're contributing to the possibility of world peace in a number of ways:

- You're taking responsibility (but not blame) for creating your reality with your thoughts and beliefs

- You're choosing to recognise and let go of the old beliefs that were creating judgments and low vibrational emotional reactions

- You're choosing to become more accepting of other people by recognising and releasing the source of your judgment

- You're quietening your inner critic by recognising it's just a mouthpiece for your limiting beliefs

- You're taking responsibility for everything you consume and the effect it has on your vibrational frequency

- You're consciously and deliberately Clearing low vibrations from yourself with your Clearing superpower.

- You're sharing StillFlow and the energy Clearing technique with friends and family and perhaps getting together or joining a group to Clear each other on a regular basis

- You are joining a StillFlow group to intend peaceful outcomes to personal, local or world conflicts

- You're choosing to direct your energy towards creating new positive alternatives rather than dwelling on, or fighting against, aspects of the world as it is now.

- You're moving from me & mine to an us point of view by choosing to collaborate rather than competing with others,because you recognise that they are are 'you' too

- You're recognising and listening to the infinite wisdom of your heart rather than the limitation of your head and allowing it to guide you

- You're letting go of the need to create or collaborate in dramas

- You're focusing your intention to Clear conflict worldwide.

When we do all this, we consciously choose to change our effect on the world's vibration and begin to make a major contribution to creating peace worldwide.

Interconnectedness dictates that there can be no end to it's effect.

You simply can't know exactly what the outcome will be. That depends entirely on the new reality we choose to intend.

"A single thought might change the motion of a universe"
Nikola Tesla

Please Share StillFlow
& The Peace Intention

If StillFlow resonates with you, it's up to you to share it with others. The move from the old way of thinking and being can be a tricky one, so the more the people around us who understand that everything is energy responding to our thoughts, the easier it is for all of us to begin working with that knowledge to create a very new type of world, together.

Remember though that StillFlow is not a philosophy it is a way of being. You cannot persuade other people of it's value unless you are living it and experiencing the benefits it brings. If you are living the StillFlow way other people will recognise the change in you.

You don't need to go on a course or be specially trained to share StillFlow, just explain it as best you can in your own words, discuss the difference it has made in you and pass them a copy of this little book. You can download it for a small donation at www.thePeaceIntention.org or you can buy a physical copy online at www.amazon.com or www.amazon.co.uk

StillFlow is a way for us to make real changes in our lives and to know that those changes could help solve the massive world challenges we now face, not in a generation or two but right here and now. Humanity and the Earth itself may be at a tipping point and the quicker we share the possibility and tools to create a new reality the better.

As Albert Einstein once said:

"The significant problems we face cannot be solved by the same level of thinking we were at when we created them."

We must evolve our thinking to solve the problems we are facing. StillFlow gives us that opportunity.

We all have the opportunity to share this evolution with as many people as possible as quickly as possible.

Here are just a few ways you can do that...

- ## Talk about living the StillFlow way

Don't shy away from talking openly and honestly about the changes you are making and why. Talk to anyone that shows an interest, email our friends and encourage them to check out the www.thePeaceIntention.org website, send them or buy them a copy of this book as a gift (a gift that benefits not just them but benefits the whole world).

- ### Gift this book to friends and strangers

If you can afford it why not buy a few books and give them as gifts to your friends and family or leave them on park benches or at the station or where you work or anywhere else that someone might find them and read them.

- **Use the StillFlow logo as a sign of your commitment to peace**

Symbols are powerful ways to share a message even without the use of words. The StillFlow logo was an inspired gift which came through a friend of the Peace Intention. It's a valuable tool for sharing your commitment to the Peace Intention.

Print it, wear it, share it, talk about it! The logo is freely downloadable from the website and it can be used as a way of recognising others living the StillFlow way. You can also use it as a talking point for discussing StillFlow to people new to the idea.

- **Be sure to join the Peace Intention**

  www.thepeaceintention.org

"We are the ones we have been waiting for"
June Jordan

Printed in Great Britain
by Amazon

27813778R00050